America Speaks! Real Comments Posted about
Trump for President

Michael Joshua

CONTENTS

Table of Contents

America Speaks! Real Comments posted about Trump for President

ACKNOWLEDGMENTS

To all those for and against Donald Trump for President who have posted their honest opinions online, I'd like to take this time to thank you. It was for your posts that made this book possible.

1 Introduction

I often find it fascinating when a presidential election starts and the candidates announce they are running. You always get the extremes from all parties on why they believe one person is a better candidate over another. These extremes lead to very heated debates, especially when each party has strong feelings for a particular side and has grown up with their parents preaching to them that their side, be it Republican, Democrat or Independent, is the only side to be on.

With that being said, I believe that those who are between the ages of 18-25 are the most strongly persuaded, as they have not yet had enough years of experience to really see the highs and lows of the American economy. They haven't seen a real war or if they lived through one or they were too young to understand its true meaning. Nor do they understand the depressing antics that many politicians play in the government roles. However, they are still Americans and they still have a right to vote.

Those of the ages older than 25 who have fought for our country and/or have worked enough in the workforce to realize that hard work and/or a higher education can really open doors, are the ones who are the most educated in the presidential campaigns. These are the people who listen to the debates on television and then spend at least 30 minutes afterwards discussing what was said and whether they believe it or not with their spouses prior to retiring for the evening. They don't just listen to a slandering media commercial and believe it to be true. They do more research on what the candidates stand for.

No matter what age group the voter comes from, everyone has an opinion about the presidential candidates. Some are mad. Some are funny. Some are just honest. Some are blunt. No matter the comment, this eBook includes a laundry list of actual posted comments that were made online by Americans and their opinion of the newest presidential candidate – Donald Trump.

Love him or hate him, he has an opinion on everything. He is known to be blunt, which pisses some people off and gets applauds by others. Which comment group will you relate with?

I hope you enjoy this collection of both sides of America – those who want Donald Trump to be the next US President and those who do not want to see him president. I hope you enjoy the book and it makes you think of both sides of Mr. Trump before you head out to the voters box and cast your election vote.

Best Wishes for a great future America...whomever the next President is!

Michael Joshua

2 Who is supporting Donald Trump for President

Everybody knows Donald Trump. After all, the guy has been famous for quite some time at this point. If you have been to Atlantic City, you have seen his developments reaching out of the skyline. Maybe you've stayed in one of his hotels.

Trump is intertwined in the highest social groups of New York City, and the man is no stranger to television, either. If nothing else, you at least know Trump for a few things...and his hair.

Mr. Trump rocked the political world when he announced his campaign to run for president. At first, his bid made a stir—made a little noise. Then, the engine revved. After a while, the Donald Trump campaign was going full throttle, all in the hopes to "Make America Great Again."

The media would lead you to believe that Trump is purely a spectacle – this rich guy who puts on a big show, and has no real supporters. To a lot of people, Donald Trump may just be making a lot of smoke with what could be perceived as offensive comments.

However, what people forget is that where there is smoke, there is fire. Little might the average American know is that Trump has supporters from Main Street to the Big Screen.

Three Iowa citizens vocalized their support for Trump at the Family Leadership Summit in Ames, Iowa. Trump was in attendance for a speaking engagement to a crowd of his supporters, dressed proudly with pins and t-shirts in support of the candidate. Think Progress, a political news blog which provides a forum that pushes progressive ideas and policies, was in attendance as well to get a little juice from Trump supporters.

Jim Nelle, who is the owner of a small business in Winterset, Iowa, carried around signs in support of Trump – around the auditorium as the candidate spoke, that is. Nelle has obviously got his eye on Trump when it comes to financial leadership.

"This country is so far in debt, we're losing so many jobs to foreign countries. I just think we need a business man to run the country like a business. I'm a Christian and I've always voted those issues in the past, like abortion was always big, but this election it's going to be different because if we don't have a country, what difference does it make if you're pro-abortion or anti-abortion? I just think we have to get the fiscal situation fixed first."

Business acumen and wisdom are clearly important factors for a farmer and investor from New Virginia, Iowa named David Brown. These both are reasons he voices his support for Trump as the best candidate for the Republican Party and he is not afraid to say so. Part of Trump's appeal to Brown is the fact that the candidate has never been in a public position.

It is even better that Trump has never even worked in politics. "Trump is my candidate that I'm supporting and the reason why I'm supporting him is because we're in financial throes. Nineteen trillion dollars under zero. We're not broke, we're $19 trillion past broke and I believe that he has the business acumen and wisdom to bring the nation back."

Another appeal for many Trump supporters is how the real estate mogul would be a politician who simply cannot be bought. The man already has plenty of money. Brown sees this as a plus about Trump as well.

"I think we need people that are beyond manipulation of donors and lobbyists and I do appreciate the fact that he's running with his own money and beyond manipulation of folks."

A New Hampton, Iowa guy, named Bill Raine, at the Ames, Iowa event – with his wife – is a Trump supporter because of how he bounces back, probably much the way the United States needs to bounce back from the recession.

"He's a businessman, he's not a politician. I've seen the guy broke and I see him and he's a billionaire today, so he's doing something right."

Trump's comments about illegal immigrants, particularly those of Latin America, have nearly become a trademark of his presidential campaign. These comments led Trump being scrutinized by the public for possibly being racist. His supporters, such as Nelle, stand behind him and his comments.

"They're illegal immigrants, they should come through legally. He says there's a lot of great Mexican people and there are. He says they're smarter than our leaders and they are. So he's not saying anything against Mexican people. He's saying they should come over legally and not illegally and the criminals should be sent back."

Nelle makes a good point about taking a closer look at Trump's word choices when giving a proper interpretation. Think Progress found much the same sentiment with others as they did with Raine from New Hampton and his thoughts on the immigration situation.

This Trump supporter clearly pulls from experience. "Where I come from, the area, we have a lot of illegals. They work on a lot of hog farms. So I've got my feelings there. I don't think that he's that completely off-key."[1]

Charlotte Laws, the author of *Rebel in High Heels*, published online an engaging opinion piece on what life is like as a Trump supporter. In "Confessions of a Closet Trump Supporter," Laws opens up her opinionated piece with asking her mother and her husband which candidate they supported.

They each answered: "Donald Trump." Laws was surprised and thrilled at the same time that she had found other Trump supporters and that these others were so close.

Laws uses this platform to discuss the struggles with being a Trump supporter. "It is socially unacceptable to support Trump; I am blasted from all directions." She goes on to admit her support for Trump in more concrete terms. "I have been a closet Trump supporter for the past two months."

Laws has Trump's back when it comes to the political firestorm that came on the heels of Trump's word choices during a debate. The entire world heard about Trump's comment to Fox news anchor Megyn Kelly. Laws supports Trump and even goes as far as commenting on how the presidential hopeful is misperceived.

"It is not sexist to insult both men and women, or to be an equal opportunity critic. It is sexist to chastise only males. Feminism is not about placing a woman on a pedestal like a fragile figurine. It is about true equality, even if on gets splattered with mud from time to time. The 'political correctness police' seem to think it is misogynistic to attack a female's appearance, yet acceptable to ridicule Donald Trump's hair."

The entertaining part of Laws' "Confessions of a Closet Trump Supporter" is when she talks about the way Trump addresses an audience. It is no secret that if nothing else, Trump is honest and is willing to stand in his own convictions even if nobody else agrees with him.

For Laws, she compares this to a "mack truck" and, like many of his supporters, will refer to it as "Trump-talk." "It is a language of its own and can require grasping the gist of a statement rather than language rather than hanging on every word."

Charlotte Laws' support for Trump, written out in a piece like "Confessions of a Closer Trump Supporter," shows how many Trump supporters there really must be. Currently, Trump's fans face possible backlash for admitting to being supporters, and many even go as far as really only seeming to exist collectively on the internet. However, what would be more interesting than an immigrant who supports Trump? Say it isn't so, but such a person does exist. [2]

Even with his perceived negative comments about immigration and its practices in the United States, a Eugene Spektar has spoken out in support for the presidential hopeful. Unfortunately, Spektar's nation of origin is not immediate evident in his posting "I am a socially liberal, millennial immigrant – and here's why Donald Trump has my vote."

Most people probably never thought they'd see a title like that in their life. Let's face it: the words 'Donald Trump,' 'immigrants,' and 'vote' do not typically share the same space in a supportive way. For this immigrant, however, Trump's wealth along is attractive. "Ironically, it is Trump's extensive wealth that gives him the unique opportunity to change the broken system."

It is no secret that Trump's wealth is working in his favor to many people. While Trump is the product of generational wealth – having a wealthy father and all – he is commended for taking the wealth his father did build and turning it into a billion dollar empire. To a lot of people, this alone is a pure sign of intelligence.

This is leadership. This is what the United States needs: take what we already have and turn it into something great. Make lemons into lemonade, if you will. This has totally convinced Spektar: "Nevertheless, Trump has convinced me that he will provide the necessary leadership to help our country succeed."

Donald Trump, if nothing else, will be remembered for shaking things up. He is proposing change and has already been a part of change when it comes to the campaign trail with how he addresses certain issues. Spektar, however, sees Trump as a multidimensional character with a story behind him that can benefit everyone.

"His urban upbringing gives me hope that he might actually fight for compromise on common sense issues, such as stricter gun control, women's health issues, increasing opportunities for the poor by taking jobs back from overseas and reforming the H-1B visa program."

Spektar goes on to express positive sentiments in Trump and his ability to be the needed change in Washington D.C.: "With Congress's approval ratings at sustained lows and polarization at abysmal highs, we need a drastic change in Washington. I believe Donald J. Trump as president could be that change." [3]

Americans involved in various levels of politics have expressed their support for Donald Trump. Doing this should definitely be considered admirable, as we live in such a society of seclusion – a society where who you associated with or who you choose to support can have an effect on your personal image. While Senator Rand Paul is one politician who credits Trump's rise to a quick "loss of sanity," other republicans disagree and support Trump.

A Republican National Committee member named Steve Duprey understands why Trump gets passed over as a serious candidate for president. However, Duprey sees the light that is Trump and is supportive of it. "There are people who think his candidacy is a flash in the pan or a flash in the moment, but I think that underestimates his appeal."

Mike Nudelman of the *Business Insider* wrote "He's not going away: Here's the fuel behind the Donald Trump rocket ship." Duprey's comments are mentioned in the article, as are those of a focus group full of Trump fans in New Hampshire. A woman, who is unnamed, in the focus group only sees the truth in what Donald Trump says.

"He says it like it is. He speaks the truth. When he talks about especially immigration control and the border, he doesn't care what people think. He tells the truth, what we need to do."

Another focus group participant spoke highly of Trump's blunt style of rhetoric. The contrast of it with many other politicians on the issues of today is appealing. "The way I see it: The political rhetoric – most of the politicians – talk in let's say pastel colors. They talk for two hours and you go away saying, 'What did they say of substance?' Probably nothing. But they haven't offended anybody and tried to make everybody their friend. Well, if they're pastel, Donald Trump is vivid colors, because he says things the way they are."

Believe it or not, former President Reagan came up in this focus group of Trump fans. This supporter too sees Trump as having the qualities the country needs to get back on track with being great again. "I like this roughness. A little Reaganesque comes to mind. Just tough. We need someone tough."

Another participant in the focus group was asked what a Trump presidency would look like. The person responded in one simple word: "classy." *Bloomberg* journalist John Heilemann, who conducted the focus group, reflects in the article what he learned from the entire experience of interacting with Trump supporters.
Trump's numbers in terms of the polls and his command of the republican vote are discussed, as well as his factually popularity versus his public persona. After, Heilemann adds: "The support for The Donald on display among the supporters I met was striking for its depth and intensity." However, the support for Donald Trump politically goes far higher, and deeper, than focus groups and journalist. [4]

Remember Sarah Palin? Oh sure you do. In 2008, then-governor of Alaska was everywhere – literally. If you missed her on the cover of *Times*, you saw her on your local news. The vice-presidential debate, hosted by Gwen Eiffel, had enough fireworks between Palin and Joe Biden that anyone who watched just three minutes of the debate was sucked in by Palin. She was entertaining. She stood in her own convictions. She refused to back down.

Who else do you know that is watching Russia from their house? Do you have any friends named Six-Pack Joe? Probably not. And these are things which make Palin all the more entertaining. Even beyond these attributes, how many politicians do you hear about from Alaska? Don't think too hard – the list is probably short.

There are a lot of things that can be said about Sarah Palin. Well, now one of the things is that the Alaskan political trailblazer is a full-blown Donald Trump fan. To some, this may come as a shock. However, to many, this will be right on par for what we all know and love Sarah Palin for.

In late August of 2015, Palin's love for Trump hit the news big time. One of the ways in which this happened was an article published online by *The Guardian*, titled "Sarah Palin showers Donald Trump with adoration in 'interview of the years."

In a nutshell, anytime Sarah Palin does an interview or major television appearance, it is big news. She knows just what to say to get people moving, and has used her knack to show her support of Donald Trump.

It seems as if her heart and beliefs are with the man – the Trump – creating all that smoke. "I've seen it since the day he made the sacrifice to hit the campaign trail; voters crave the anti-status quo politician. They want results. They need someone to fire all the politically correct police. This is a movement."

To say the amount of traction Trump is gaining is a "movement" would have to be an understatement. In fact, during this very same interview, it struck Palin to practice a little of that French she learned in high school. "Everything about Donald Trump's campaign is….avant-garde."

Palin acknowledges Trump's accomplishments in the polls. "He is crushing it in the polls," the politician said in the interview, before stressing how Trump is actually talking to the American people rather than talking at them. "Viewers...he's talking to you. He wants to connect with those who are showing up at the polls."

It is no secret that the economy is not exactly what every United States citizen wishes it were. At least, if you were around in the 1990s you know it sure is not what it used to be. Of course, this is one of the main points of Donald Trump's campaign.

The real estate mogul wants to "Make America Great Again," which means fixing a broken system and an economy that relies too heavily on outsourced good and services while its own people go underemployed or without work altogether. Palin sees how Trump can insert a little of his business-savvy magic into the situation. When discussing economic growth statistics by the Commerce Department, Palin sees straight through what is really going on.

"I don't think we're getting the true state of the economy out of the White House. So thanks for setting that straight."

Trump's claim to want to create a simplified tax code? Palin is onboard with that. She wants fairness just like the New York-native Trump does. When asked about the incident between Trump and Univision anchor Jorge Ramos – an incident on national television where Trump told the Hispanic-American to "go back to his country" – Palin is standing by her man yet again.

"You schooled that radical activist and it was the right thing to do, because I don't think he's going to pull that again. Where do you get your guts for that kind of necessary confrontation?"

Who knows? With Palin's say-it-how-you-mean-it demeanor and her lack of fear for standing up for what she believes in, the Alaskan could very well be good support for Trump, especially getting closer to the finish line. If anything, Sarah Palin knows how to get attention and get people to listen: a lot like Trump. [5]

When it comes to the celebrity world, your image can make or break your career. This gives all the more reasons for folks in the entertainment industry to maybe shy away from Trump. Much like Charlotte Laws, if your career and livelihood depends on your image, you might be more inclined to be a closet Trump supporter.

On the contrary, however, there sure-enough are celebrity Trump supporters – celebrities who are not afraid to stick up for the Trump. Star power can go a long way, even when it comes to politics.

Without a doubt, it would surprise a lot to know that the very eccentric Dennis Rodman has come out as a Donald Trump supporter. The former NBA star, who played for the Detroit Pistons, San Antonio Spurs, Chicago Bulls, Los Angeles Lakers, and the Dallas Mavericks during his career, has long been known for strange piercings, tattoos, and even multicolored hair.

Well, Rodman pronounced his support for Trump early in 2015 via Twitter, and it looks like the former NBA star likes Trump because the real estate mogul is not a politician: "@realDonaldTrump has been a great friend for many years. We don't need another politician, we need a businessman like Mr. Trump! Trump 2016"

Speaking of the Dallas Mavericks, Mark Cuban, who is the owner of the sports team, supports the Trump. The *Shark Tank* investor apparently likes Trump's brash and confident approach to politics. Cuban is quoted as saying that Trump is "the best thing to happen to politics in a long, long time." In another interview, Cuban spoke highly of Trump's transparency: "....says what's on his mind. He gives honest answers rather than prepared answers." [6]

When it comes to sports players, it looks like Donald Trump might have quite a following, even if they are closeted. Terrell Owens, who is known for having quite the star power on and off the field, supports Trump. The former NFL player played for the San Francisco 49ers, Philadelphia Eagles, Dallas Cowboys, Buffalo Bills, and Cincinnati Bengals during his time in the league and has come out as a Donald Trump supporter as well.

This may or may not be a surprise, considering Owens himself is a contestant of "The Apprentice." TMZ reported Owens as saying, "This may be what the country needs and Trump...he's a guy who won't put up with B.S. and has what it takes to change how government is run."

Owens later added, ironically paralleling his words with what you might here from Trump: "With that being said, Trump... YOU'RE HIRED." [7]

Many people might not know what to expect from a star like Omarosa Manigault-Stallworth, who simply is known as Omarosa. She first rose to fame on Donald Trump's "Celebrity Apprentice" and is known for being quite the business savvy woman. Low and behold, Omarosa, who is known for being a "die-hard registered Democrat," defended the Trump.

In fact, she even called him the "Tiger Woods of politics." Omarosa is quoted as saying: "When Tiger got involved with golf, people who had never been watching or involved or interested in golf, they got engaged. That's what's happening with this Trump candidacy." Omarosa? Go figure!

You can go ahead and add the former pro-wrestler Jesse Ventura, who went on to be governor of Minnesota, to the list of those with star power showing full support for Donald Trump to take ahold of the 2016 presidential seat. And as one might expect, when professing his support for Trump, things could get a little physical.

Ventura, when speaking on the Trump as an independent, said he would "like somebody else to win overall. You know what, as far as republicans are concerned, I said I hope Trump wins." Evidentially, if nothing else, Ventura likes Trump more than any of the other republican contenders for the presidential seat.

For those who remember the 1970s, the name Ted Nugent might ring a bell. The singer was very popular in that era, mostly for his songs "Stranglehold," "Cat Scratch Fever," "Wango Tango," and "Great White Buffalo." The lead guitarist of 1960s group Amboy Dukes, whose hit "Journey to the Center of the Mind" is still popular to this day, has now added to his repertoire being a Trump supporter.

In his commentary about the Trump, Nugent is clearly not only a fan of Trump's tactics, but is also keeping what America needs in mind. Nugent is quoted as saying that Trump as president would "kick ass and take names, and that's what America needs right now."[8]

Probably the biggest name in Hollywood to come out of the Trump supporters' closet, as Charlotte Laws called the group, would be the very high profiled Clint Eastwood. Rather than Eastwood coming out and professing his support, he has taken another more solidified approach: letting his actions speak louder than his words.

In July 2015, Trump's tweet showed Eastwood's support: "I will be in California this weekend making a speech for Clint Eastwood. Then to Arizona and Vegas. Big crowds. Discussing illegals and more!" This particular event with Eastwood was described by a Trump campaign spokeswoman as "private." Therefore little information was made available about it. Nonetheless, the fact that Eastwood would allow and even invite Trump to speak says a lot. [9]

3 Reasons why to vote for Trump for President

The following was from an anonymous source who wants to remain anonymous, for many reasons. Instead of including different sources for this section, I decided that this one source hits upon all topics that are important to a presidential candidate, and therefore, just numbered the actual points within the content.

"The criticisms of Trump are amazingly missing something.

They are lacking in negative stories from those who work for him or have had business dealings with him. After all the employees he's had and all the business deals he's made there is a void of criticism. In fact, long term employees call him a strong and merciful leader and say he is far more righteous and of high integrity than people may think.

And while it may surprise many, he's actually humble when it comes to his generosity and kindness. A good example is a story that tells of his limo breaking down on a deserted highway outside of New York City. A middle-aged couple stopped to help him and as a thank you he paid off their mortgage, but he didn't brag about that. Generous and good people rarely talk of charity they bestow on others.

But as much as all this is interesting, the real thing that people want to know is what Donald Trump's plan is for America. It's funny how so many people say they don't know what it is, or they act like Trump is hiding it. The information is readily available if people would just do a little homework. But, since most Americans won't do their own research, here, in no particular order, is an overview of many of Trumps positions and plans:

1.) Trump believes that America should not intervene militarily in other country's problems without being compensated for doing so. If America is going to risk the lives of our soldiers and incur the expense of going to war, then the nations we help must be willing to pay for our help. Using the Iraq War as an example, he cites the huge monetary expense to American taxpayers (over $1.5 trillion, and possibly much more depending on what sources are used to determine the cost) in addition to the cost in human life.

He suggests that Iraq should have been required to give us enough of their oil to pay for the expenses we incurred. He includes in those expenses the medical costs for our military and $5 million for each family that lost a loved one in the war and $2 million for each family of soldiers who received severe injuries.

2.) Speaking of the military, Trump wants America to have a strong military again. He believes the single most important function of the federal government is national defense. He has said he wants to find the General Patton or General MacArthur that could lead our military buildup back to the strength it needs to be.

While he hasn't said it directly that I know of, Trump's attitude about America and about winning tells me he'd most likely be quick to eliminate rules of engagement that handicap our military in battle. Clearly Trump is a "win at all costs" kind of guy, and I'm sure that would apply to our national defense and security, too.

3.) Trump wants a strong foreign policy and believes that it must include 7 core principles (which seem to support my comment in the last point):

American interests come first. Always. No apologies.
Maximum firepower and military preparedness.
Only go to war to win.

Stay loyal to your friends and suspicious of your enemies.
Keep the technological sword razor sharp.
See the unseen. Prepare for threats before they materialize.
Respect and support our present and past warriors.

4.) Trump believes that terrorists who are captured should be treated as military combatants, not as criminals like the Obama administration treats them.

5.) Trump makes the point that China's manipulation of their currency has given them unfair advantage in our trade dealings with them. He says we must tax their imports to offset their currency manipulation, which will cause American companies to be competitive again and drive manufacturing back to America and create jobs here.

Although he sees China as the biggest offender, he believes that America should protect itself from all foreign efforts to take our jobs and manufacturing. For example, Ford is building a plant in Mexico and Trump suggests that every part or vehicle Ford makes in Mexico be taxed 35% if they want to bring it into the U. S., which would cause companies like Ford to no longer be competitive using their Mexican operations and move manufacturing back to the U. S., once again creating jobs here.

6.) Trump wants passage of NOPEC legislation (No Oil Producing and Exporting Cartels Act – NOPEC – S.394), which would allow the government to sue OPEC for violating antitrust laws. According to Trump, that would break up the cartel. He also wants to unleash our energy companies to drill domestically (sound like Sarah Palin's drill baby, drill?) thereby increasing domestic production creating jobs and driving domestic costs of oil and gas down while reducing dependence on foreign oil.

7.) Trump believes a secure border is critical for both security and prosperity in America. He wants to build a wall to stop illegals from entering put controls on immigration. (And he says he'll get Mexico to pay for the wall, which many have scoffed at, but given his business successes I wouldn't put it past him.) He also wants to enforce our immigration laws and provide no path to citizenship for illegals.

8.) Trump wants a radical change to the tax system to not only make it better for average Americans, but also to encourage businesses to stay here and foreign businesses to move here. The resulting influx of money to our nation would do wonders for our economy.

He wants to make America the place to do business. He also wants to lower the death tax and the taxes on capital gains and dividends. This would put more than $1.6 trillion back into the economy and help rebuild the 1.5 million jobs we've lost to the current tax system.

He also wants to charge companies who outsource jobs overseas a 20% tax, but for those willing to move jobs back to America they would not be taxed. And for citizens he has a tax plan that would allow Americans to keep more of what they earn and spark economic growth. He wants to change the personal income tax to:

Up to $30,000 taxed at 1%
From $30,000 to $100,000 taxed at 5%
From $100,000 to $1,000,000 taxed at 10%
$1,000,000 and above taxed at 15%

9.) Trump wants Obamacare repealed. He says it's a "job-killing, health care-destroying monstrosity" that "can't be reformed, salvaged, or fixed." He believes in allowing real competition in the health insurance marketplace to allow competition to drive prices down. He also believes in tort reform to get rid of defensive medicine and lower costs.

10.) Trump wants spending reforms in Washington, acknowledging that America spends far more than it receives in revenue. He has said he believes that if we don't stop increasing the national debt once it hits $24 trillion it will be impossible to save this country.

11.) Even though he says we need to cut spending, he does not want to harm those on Medicare, Medicaid, or Social Security. He believes that the citizens have faithfully paid in to the system to have these services available and that the American government has an obligation to fulfill its end of the bargain and provide those benefits.

Therefore, he wants to build the economy up so that we have the revenue to pay those costs without cutting the benefits to the recipients. He disagrees with Democrats who think raising taxes is the answer and says that when you do that you stifle the economy.

On the other hand, when you lower taxes and create an environment to help businesses they will grow, hire more workers, and those new workers will be paying taxes that become more tax revenue for the government.

12.) Trump also wants reform of the welfare state saying that America needs "a safety net, not a hammock." He believes in a welfare to work program that would help reduce the welfare rolls and encourage people to get back to work. And he wants a crackdown on entitlement fraud.

13.) Trump believes climate change is a hoax.

14.) Trump opposes Common Core.

15.) Trump is pro-life, although he allows for an exception due   to rape, incest, or the life of the mother.

16.) Trump is pro 2nd Amendment rights.

17.) Trump's view on same-sex marriage is that marriage is between a man and a woman, but he also believes that this is a states' rights issue, not a federal issue.

18.) Trump supports the death penalty.
Trump believes that there is a lack of common sense, innovative thinking in Washington (Hmmm... looks like he believes in horse sense!). He says it's about seeing the unseen and that's the kind of thinking we need to turn this country around. He tells a personal story to illustrate the point:

"When I opened Trump National Golf Club at Rancho Palos Verdes in Los Angeles, I was immediately told that I would need to build a new and costly ballroom. The current ballroom was gorgeous, but it only sat 200 people and we were losing business because people needed a larger space for their events. Building a new ballroom would take years to get approval and permits (since it's on the Pacific Ocean), and cost about $5 million. I took one look at the ballroom and saw immediately what needed to be done. The problem wasn't the size of the room, it was the size of the chairs.

They were huge, heavy, and unwieldy. We didn't need a bigger ballroom, we needed smaller chairs! So I had them replaced with high-end, smaller chairs. I then had our people sell the old chairs and got more money for them than the cost of the new chairs. In the end, the ballroom went from seating 200 people to seating 320 people. Our visitors got the space they desired, and I spared everyone the hassle of years of construction and $5 million of expense. It's amazing what you can accomplish with a little common sense."

On top of his saving years of construction and $5 million in expenses, he also was able to keep the ballroom open for business during the time it would have been under remodeling, which allowed him to continue to make money on the space instead of losing that revenue during construction time.
Donald Trump's entire life has been made up of success and winning.

He's been accused of bankruptcies, but that's not true. He's never filed personal bankruptcy. He's bought companies and legally used bankruptcy laws to restructure their debt, just as businesses do all the time. But he's never been bankrupt personally.

He's a fighter that clearly loves America and would fight for our nation.

Earlier I quoted Trump saying, "I love America. And when you love something, you protect it passionately – fiercely, even." We never hear that from Democrats or even from most Republicans. Donald Trump is saying things that desperately need to be said but no other candidate has shown the fortitude to stand up and say them.

Looking over this list of what he wants for America I see a very necessary set of goals that are long past due. Before we criticize someone because the media does, maybe we should seriously consider what he has to offer."

4 Reasons why not to vote for Trump for President

In this section, I specifically state the sources that made the comment. Albeit that the content within this eBook is only a part of the entire comment made by the poster, I tried to capture the actual point they were trying to make without it being too lengthy. If you would like to read their entire post, you can find all quoted sources below in the "Why Wouldn't You Vote for Donald Trump for President" discussion on Quora. [10]

Trump was a registered Democrat (2001-2009) and in favor of abortion rights, saying that he was "very pro-choice"; he said that Bill Clinton was one of our best presidents and gushed over Hillary calling her a "fantastic senator"; he called himself "very liberal when it comes to health care" and that he believes in "universal healthcare"; he was in favor of increased gun control and banning assault rifles and imposing longer waiting periods before purchase; he called for a one-time 14.25% tax on wealthy Americans; and he has argued for legalizing drugs. *Kim Petersen, Former Bush41/DoD/Senate staffer & SpecOps alum*

The difference between business and politics is that, in the private sector workplace, being a bully works most of the time. Sometimes, it backfires, but on the whole, putting fear into your enemies is a way to get ahead in the corporate world. In the workplace, most people are just trying to protect an income and, the higher you get, the more they have to lose.

So as a bully, you'll win more than you'll lose. International diplomacy is different. You're not dealing with people trying to protect individual careers and reputations (who can be bullied) but with people who have to appear strong to the groups that have chosen them as leaders (and who, therefore, can't be bullied as easily because their constituents expect fortitude).

Aggression and arrogance, in diplomacy, cause more problems than they solve. What works on some piss ant VP of Business Development isn't going to work on a heavyweight like Vladimir Putin. *Michael O. Church* functional programmer and machine learning engineer in Chicago.

Then here's a man willing to say that he is not eager to explain his "foolproof plan to defeat Isis" unless he is elected. He figures if he is not elected he will have to tell us eventually what the plan is, and certainly thousands of people may die before then and there will be continued terrorist threats to our allies, but hey, the man needs to get elected and that's more important, right? *Kenneth I Altman, Writer, Artist, Passport Specialist, Visa Specialist*

Donald Trump uses publicity to market his name and image. Period. That is his best claim to any sort of fame. *Paul deHolczer, History buff*

He's got too much in common with Clinton - and more of it. He makes statements that only a fool would believe without questioning them (most of which are more outrageous than 'I didn't inhale', at that), apparently thinking -- *assuming*, even -- that I'm a big enough fool to

not question them. Or he thinks that somehow I owe him to not question them because he's who he is and I'm merely who I am.
Michael Forrest Jones

He says in his many books that if you want to become an ultra successful person, you have to think big, lead yourself, and work your butt off. Nobody's going to disagree with that.

It all sounds fantastic, he speaks frankly and matter of factly compared to his Republican competitors and his message is relatively well-crafted this time around.

But he has so much going against him that he probably won't stand a chance once the attack ads begin:
Four years ago, he tried to advocate the birther movement and allegedly had "solid evidence" that proved that Obama wasn't born in the U.S. That was likely nothing more than a publicity stunt and it was a huge blow to his credibility at the time. That's a mistake no serious contender for President should make publicly with the grandiosity of a used car salesperson.

Could you really picture him uniting the nation during times of tragedy like mass shootings and terrorist attacks? A frank and straight-shooting disposition can only take you so far when people want to know that you genuinely care and you can be emotionally impacted just like the rest of us.

Can you accurately predict the ramifications of his proposed "take it or leave it" foreign policy? Can he really build a wall on the Mexican border and make Mexico pay for it? How would he accomplish this and does it make rational sense? Think about that before you pull a lever for him.

Did you see the way he demeaned the winners of his past seasons of *The Apprentice* who were working for him at the time that show was airing? Why was it necessary to treat his employees like crap on national television? Do you aspire to be like that?

Many other billionaires like Richard Branson, Oprah Winfrey and Bill Gates can accomplish their goals without being so overtly nasty with people. What excuse is there for behavior like that?

For the past several years, he's televised "serious" boardroom meetings with the likes of Gury Busey, Dennis Rodman and Gilbert Gottfriend. He actually played a "mediator" for these celebrities when they had conflicts with each other and theatrically reprimanded these folks on camera for not making sound business decisions. Do you really consider this a prerequisite to become President of the United States? *Tim Enalls, Founder of IdeaGenius.com and StartupOasis.com*

He's been willing to speak in platitudes - "Make America Great Again!" - and he's been willing to sling mud - the unabashed engagement with the "where's Obama's birth certificate" crowd - but he hasn't talked policy yet, and that's in twenty-seven years of publicly waffling about whether or not to run for the highest office in the land. In close to three decades of semi-public life, we should know something about the political positions of a person, and with Trump, what we know is the following:

- He is willing to tell CPAC that he is anti-gun control and anti-abortion - but there's no track record of action actually backing that up
- He is against a Trans Pacific Partnership of free trade.
- He wants to take a firmer hand with OPEC.

That's three decades' worth of Trump's semi-political career for you. Three decades and all I could come up with were three bullet points, none of which are remotely serious policy recommendations: one is an assertion lacking evidence, one is simply an automatic gainsaying of the current president, and one is the easiest way of playing to the crowds who want cheaper gas (i.e. everyone). *Harold Kingsberg*

Donald Trump is not Presidential. He's a vindictive, wrongheaded, thin skinned blowhard who responds childishly to criticism and would be a diplomatic nightmare as President.

If he was smart, as you claim, he would keep his mouth shut more often and would have better comebacks. Everyone who disagrees with him is a loser. The dude seems wholly incapable of compromise or of even considering opinions other than his own.

He's successful and driven, but it's easier to make money when you start with money and he started off with a lot. He took over his father's real estate business in his mid twenties (I think) and has done really well, but he lucked into the opportunity.

And he's been pussyfooting around running for president FOREVER, so who knows how sincere he is, or if it matters. *Anonymous*

5 Conclusion

It looks like Donald Trump just might be here to stay, possibly even as president of the United States. The New York-native may indeed be on the receiving end of a lot of political backlash, particularly in the recent months. However, all of this does not seem to be slowing him down the least bit. In fact, if nothing else, it could be building the Trump up to be a bigger, better, and badder force than anyone could have ever imagined.

One thing is for sure: Trump has supporters in basically all walks of life, whether anyone wants to admit it or not – whether the media will let such a thing be seen or not or just lead the not-so-free-thinking world to think that Trump is just out there making noise.

It is very clear that the real estate mogul is doing much more than simply making noise and creating smoke. Trump has support from political allies, which would definitely help in the realm of politics. Sarah Palin could very well be the biggest and loudest of them all if you step back and look at it.

As unlikely as it may seem, Trump has even managed to earn the support of a "socially liberal, millennial immigrant" in the wake of his controversial comments about immigration in the United States. All the way down on Main Street, be it in Iowa with three everyday Americans, or just normal folk taking part in a New Hampshire focus group, there are people who have Trump's back. Closet Trump supporters, as writer Charlotte Laws calls them in her "confession," are creeping up in every nook and cranny of the United States.

Trump has his own star power, but the star power of the likes of sports players Dennis Rodman and Terrell Owens sure adds a little umph to the campaign trail. Fellow business owners and political elites like Omarosa, Mark Cuban, and Jesse Ventura further show that more and more people are slowly seeing what Donald Trump is bringing to the table.

When it comes to the entertainment industry, the likes of Ted Nugent and the infamous Clint Eastwood further stir the pot with their well-earned star power to show that the Trump is much more than simply entertainment. Where there is smoke, there is fire. And Donald Trump, the man who has appeared from the smoke, has plenty of support from every walk of life – more support than the media would lead anyone to believe.

In conclusion, I hope this eBook has aroused some type of reaction from you. I'm not sure after reading all this is if you will or will not vote for Donald Trump for President, but I hope it has shed some light on both sides of him.

Obviously, the best thing to do is to avoid slandering media attacks for any political figure and just follow the Presidential debate on television each time it is aired to make an educated decision. Most Presidents in the past have had some flaw or another, so I think it's safe to say that Donald Trump has his flaws as well, but does it make him any lesser of a candidate?

Just do America a favor...use your right to vote and make it count. Vote for who you believe will help America the best in all aspects of the Presidential job.

God Bless America and Let Freedom Ring!

6 Footnotes

1. http://thinkprogress.org/election/2015/07/20/3682386/trump-supporters-iowa/
2. http://dailycaller.com/2015/08/27/confessions-of-a-closet-trump-supporter/
3. http://qz.com/490560/a-millennial-immigrant-new-yorker-explains-why-donald-trump-represents-him/
4. http://www.businessinsider.com/who-are-donald-trumps-supporters-2015-7
5. http://www.theguardian.com/us-news/2015/aug/29/sarah-palin-donald-trump-interview
6. http://thehill.com/blogs/in-the-know/250966-celebs-line-up-for-against-donald-trump
7. http://blacksportsonline.com/home/2015/06/terrell-owens-on-donald-trump-running-for-president/
8. http://thehill.com/blogs/in-the-know/250966-celebs-line-up-for-against-donald-trump
9. http://www.thepoliticalinsider.com/director-clint-eastwood-just-made-a-huge-announcement-about-donald-trump/#ixzz3kehyIh7Z
10. http://www.quora.com/U-S-Politics/Why-wouldnt-you-vote-for-Donald-Trump-for-president

7 One last thing…

If you enjoyed this book or found it useful, I'd be very grateful if you'd post a short review on Amazon. Your support really does make a difference and I read all the reviews personally so I can get your feedback and make this book even better.

If you'd like to leave a review then all you need to do is click the review link on the book's page on Amazon here:

Thanks again for your support!

ABOUT THE AUTHOR

Michael Joshua graduated with a degree in Finance and works at a bank as a financial analyst. He enjoys keeping up with business, finance and political discussions. You can find him on Twitter:
https://twitter.com/mjoshua_author
or on Goodreads: https://www.goodreads.com/user/show/46377085-michael-joshua